The
ELLESMERE MANUSCRIPT
of

Chaucer's
Canterbury
Tales

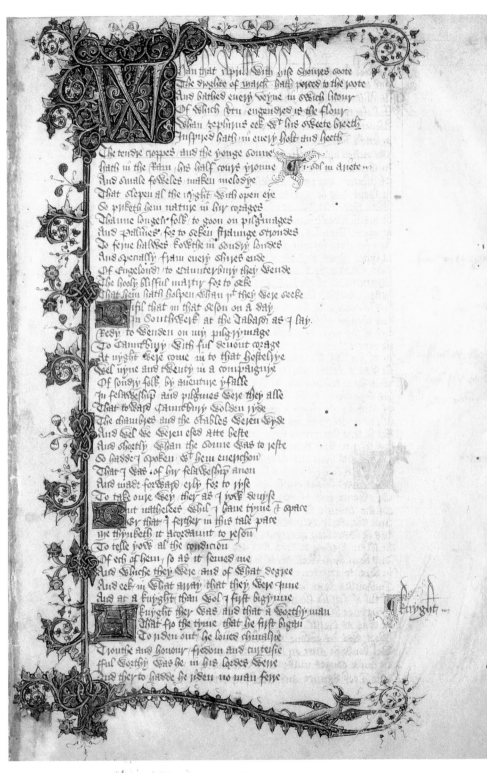

Whan that Aprill with his shoures soote
The droghte of March hath perced to the roote
And bathed every veyne in swich licour
Of which vertu engendred is the flour
Whan Zephirus eek with his sweete breeth
Inspired hath in every holt and heeth
The tendre croppes and the yonge sonne
Hath in the Ram his half cours yronne [Sol in Ariete]
And smale foweles maken melodye
That slepen al the nyght with open eye
So priketh hem nature in hir corages
Thanne longen folk to goon on pilgrimages
And palmeres for to seken straunge strondes
To ferne halwes kowthe in sondry londes
And specially from every shires ende
Of Engelond to Caunterbury they wende
The hooly blisful martir for to seke
That hem hath holpen whan that they were seeke
Bifil that in that seson on a day
In Southwerk at the Tabard as I lay
Redy to wenden on my pilgrymage
To Caunterbury with ful devout corage
At nyght was come in to that hostelrye
Wel nyne and twenty in a compaignye
Of sondry folk by aventure yfalle
In felaweshipe and pilgrimes were they alle
That toward Caunterbury wolden ryde
The chambres and the stables weren wyde
And wel we weren esed atte beste
And shortly whan the sonne was to reste
So hadde I spoken with hem everichon
That I was of hir felaweshipe anon
And made forward erly for to ryse
To take oure wey ther as I yow devyse
But nathelees whil I have tyme and space
Er that I ferther in this tale pace
Me thynketh it acordaunt to resoun
To telle yow al the condicioun
Of ech of hem so as it semed me
And whiche they were and of what degree
And eek in what array that they were inne
And at a knyght than wol I first bigynne [Knyght]
A Knyght ther was and that a worthy man
That fro the tyme that he first bigan
To riden out he loved chivalrie
Trouthe and honour fredom and curteisie
Ful worthy was he in his lordes werre
And therto hadde he riden no man ferre

The
ELLESMERE MANUSCRIPT
of

Chaucer's Canterbury Tales

Herbert C. Schulz

Huntington Library

San Marino, California

The Ellesmere Manuscript of Chaucer's
Canterbury Tales
    Herbert C. Schulz with a bibliographical note
by Joseph A. Dane and Seth Lerer

© 1966 by the Henry E. Huntington Library
    and Art Gallery
© 1999 first hardcover edition

Library of Congress Catalog-in-Publication Data
Schulz, Herbert Clarence, 1902–
    The Ellesmere manuscript of Chaucer's
Canterbury tales / by Herbert C. Schulz.—1st
hardcover ed.
        p.   cm.
    "Bibliographical note by Joseph A. Dane and
Seth Lerer"—Cover.
    Includes bibliographical references (p.   ).
    ISBN 0-87328-152-7
    1. Chaucer, Geoffrey, d. 1400. Canterbury
tales—Criticism, Textual. 2. Chaucer, Geoffrey,
d. 1400—Manuscripts. 3. Manuscripts, English
(Middle)—California—San Marino.
4. Manuscripts, Medieval—California—San
Marino. 5. Christian pilgrims and pilgrimages in
art. 6. Ellesmere Chaucer. I. Chaucer, Geoffrey,
d. 1400. Canterbury tales. II. Henry E. Huntington
Library and Art Gallery. III. Ellesmere Chaucer.
IV. Title.
PR1875.M3S34   1998
821'.1—DC21   9837730
                    CIP

This edition was designed by Leslie Thomas Fitch.
It was created with QuarkXPress 3.32 and Adobe
Photoshop 4.0 on Macintosh computers. The
fonts used were Adobe Perpetua and Perpetua
Expert. It was printed on 170 gsm multi-art silk
at C.S. Graphics, Singapore.

Publication of this book was made possible
through the generosity of the J. B. and Emily Van
Nuys Charities.

HUNTINGTON LIBRARY PRESS
http://huntington.org/HLPress/HEHPubs.html

The flyleaves in this book are reproduced
from the first and last flyleaves of the Ellesmere
manuscript.

Contents

Introduction

To Chaucer that is floure of rethoryk
In englisshe tong and excellent poete.
—John Walton • 1410

THE ELLESMERE MANUSCRIPT of Geoffrey Chaucer's *Canterbury Tales*, commonly referred to as the "Ellesmere Chaucer," is one of the most valuable and cherished manuscripts in the Huntington Library. A similarly high opinion of it would doubtless be held by its owners were it, instead, in any other library of the English-speaking world. The reasons for this distinction readily reveal themselves and invite the attention of both the general reader with a fondness for books and literature and the student with a serious interest in the text.

Chaucer's position as the most prominent author in the history of English literature before Shakespeare has long been a well-established fact. No other text in the entire Chaucer canon can equal the *Canterbury Tales*, and indeed it would be difficult to name a single literary work of the whole medieval period, by any author, that surpasses these tales in their direct appeal to the reader. They can, with considerable assurance, be placed among the world's greatest literary achievements. Their continued vitality almost six centuries after they were first written is well attested by the several "modernizations" of the Middle English text, from Dryden to the present generation, and by repeated appearances in paperback editions.

Quod I releesse thee thy thousand pound
As thou right now were cropen out of the ground
Ne nevere er now ne haddest knowen me
For sire I wol nat taken a peny of thee
For al my craft ne noght for my travaille
Thou hast ypayed wel for my vitaille
It is ynogh and farewel have good day
And took his hors and forth he goth his way
Lordynges this question thanne wolde I aske now
Which was the mooste fre as thynketh yow
Now telleth me er that ye ferther wende
I kan namoore my tale is at an ende

Heere is ended the ffrankeleyns tale

Heere folweth the Phisiciens tale

Ther was as telleth Titus Livius
A knyght that was called Virginius
Fulfild of honour and of worthynesse
And strong of freendes and of greet richesse
This knyght a doghter hadde by his wyf
No children hadde he mo in al his lyf
Fair was this mayde in excellent beautee
Aboven every wight that man may see
For nature hath with soverayn diligence
Yformed hir in so greet excellence
As though she wolde seyn lo I nature
Thus kan I forme and peynte a creature
Whan that me list who kan me countrefete
Pigmalion noght though he ay forge and bete
Or grave or peynte for I dar wel seyn
Apelles Zanzis sholde werche in veyn
Outher to grave or peynte or forge or bete
If they presumed me to countrefete
For he that is the formere principal
Hath maked me his vicaire general
To forme and peynten erthely creatures
Right as me list and ech thyng in my cure is
Under the moone that may wane and waxe
And for my werk right no thyng wol I axe
My lord and I been ful of oon accord
I made hir to the worshipe of my lord
So do I alle myne othere creatures
What colour that they han or what figures

I. The Pilgrims

THE TEXT of the Ellesmere Chaucer therefore commands the highest critical respect, a virtue naturally shared with the many other manuscripts of the *Canterbury Tales*, over eighty in number, including fragments. Of the several distinctive features which contribute to the pre-eminent position of the Ellesmere manuscript in such a large group, the most notable is the series of twenty-three paintings depicting the Canterbury Pilgrims. This is the only extant manuscript which has preserved a complete graphic representation of the Pilgrims whose tales were written by Chaucer. Each Pilgrim is shown astride his horse and is placed in the margin of the page alongside the opening lines of the tale he related as the company travels from London to Canterbury. Several other Pilgrims mentioned in the General Prologue are omitted from the Ellesmere series of paintings because Chaucer never completed the ambitious project as it was originally envisaged. Speaking with the voice of Herry Bailly the Host, he had proposed that each member of the company should relate two tales on the road to Canterbury and two more on the homeward journey. Of this prodigious number only a fifth were written and have come down to us, not even sufficient for each of the Pilgrims to display his talents as a storyteller in the first round of tales.

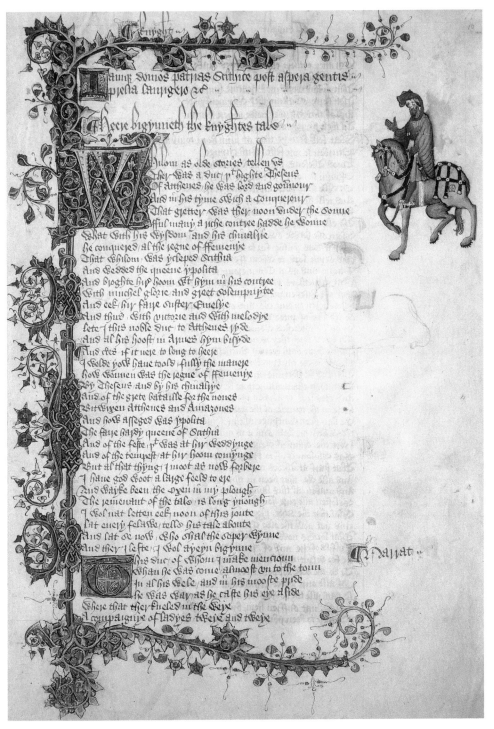

Of storial thyng that toucheth gentillesse
And eek moralitee and hoolynesse
Blameth nat me if that ye chese amys
The Millere is a cherl ye knowe wel this
So was the Reue and othere manye mo
And harlotrie they tolden bothe two
Auyseth yow putteth me out of blame
And eek men shal nat maken ernest of game

¶ Heere bigynneth the Milleres his tale ..

Whilom ther was dwellynge at Oxenford
A riche gnof that gestes heeld to bord
And of his craft he was a Carpenter
With hym ther was dwellynge a poure scoler
Hadde lerned Art but al his fantasye
Was turned for to lerne Astrologye
And koude a certeyn of conclusions
To demen by interrogacions
If þt men asked hym in certein houres
Whan þt men sholde haue droghte or elles shoures
Or if men asked hym what sholde bifalle
Of euery thyng I may nat rekene hem alle
This clerk was cleped hende Nicholas
Of derne loue he koude and of solas
And ther to he was sleigh and ful priue
And lyk a mayden meke for to se
A chambre hadde he in that hostelrye
Allone with outen any compaignye
Ful fetisly ydight with herbes soote
And he hym self as sweete as is the roote
Of lycorys or any Cetewale
His Almageste and bookes grete and smale
His Astrelabie longynge for his Art
Hise Augrym stones layen faire a part
On shelues couched at his beddes heed
His presse ycouered with a faldyng reed
And al aboue ther lay a gay Sautrie
On which he made a nyghtes melodie
So swetely that al the chambre rong
And Angelus ad virginem he song
And after that he song the kynges noote
Ful often blessed was his myrie throte
And thus this sweete clerk his tyme spente
After his freendes fyndyng and his rente
This Carpenter hadde wedded newe a wyf
Which that he louede moore than his lyf

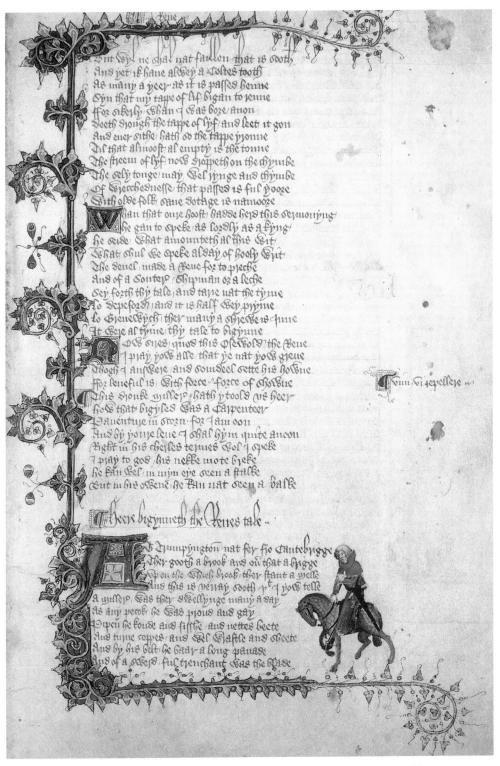

But if ne shal nat fallen that is sooth,
And yet ik have alwey a coltes tooth
As many a yeer as it is passed henne
Syn that my tappe of lyf bigan to renne
For sikerly whan I was bore anon
Deeth drough the tappe of lyf and leet it gon
And ever sithe hath so the tappe yronne
Til that almoost al empty is the tonne
The streem of lyf now droppeth on the chymbe
The sely tonge may wel rynge and chymbe
Of wrecchednesse that passed is ful yoore
With olde folk save dotage is namoore

Whan that oure hoost hadde herd this sermonyng
He gan to speke as lordly as a kyng
He seide what amounteth al this wit
What shul we speke alday of hooly writ
The devel made a reve for to preche
And of a souter shipman or a leche
Sey forth thy tale and tarie nat the tyme
Lo depeford and it is half wey pryme
Lo grenewych ther many a shrewe is inne
It were al tyme thy tale to bigynne

Now sires quod this Osewold the reve
I pray yow alle that ye nat yow greve
Thogh I answere and somdeel sette his howve
For leveful is with force force of showve
This dronke millere hath ytoold us heer
How that bigyled was a carpenteer
Paraventure in scorn for I am oon
And by youre leve I shal hym quite anoon
Right in his cherles termes wol I speke
I pray to god his nekke mote breke
He kan wel in myn eye seen a stalke
But in his owene he kan nat seen a balke

Heere bigynneth the Reves tale

At Trumpyngton nat fer fro Cantebrigge
Ther gooth a brook and over that a brigge
Upon the whiche brook ther stant a melle
And this is verray sooth that I yow telle
A millere was ther dwellynge many a day
As any pecok he was proud and gay
Pipen he koude and fisshe and nettes beete
And turne coppes and wel wrastle and sheete
And by his belt he baar a long panade
And of a swerd ful trenchaunt was the blade

Had Chaucer been able to fulfill his promise, the wealth of stories that would have enriched early English literature can readily be imagined. Among the most entertaining would have been the Reeve's fourth tale, with its attempted rout of the Miller as the feud between the two at last came to its conclusion, for Chaucer has warned us in the General Prologue description of the Reeve that he was a man very difficult to outwit. A militant second prologue by that authority on the delicate question of matrimonial sovereignty, the Wife of Bath, berating the Merchant for his biased stand on the matter, could well have launched a collateral feud between these natural antagonists. And we may feel certain, since nothing to the contrary can now be maintained, that Chaucer's relation of the final "soper at our aller cost" awarded to the Pilgrim "that bereth him beste of alle" would have been one of the most convivial pages in the entire work. But had this colossal plan been completed, there would probably have been no Ellesmere Chaucer!

Among the Pilgrims whose portraits will not be found in the Ellesmere manuscript is the Plowman. Thirteen lines in the General Prologue provide a sympathetic characterization which instantly captures our respect and holds high promise for the tale which Chaucer apparently never wrote. Perhaps for this reason two entirely unrelated "Plowman's Tales" were included along with the authentic *Canterbury Tales* during earlier centuries. One of these is the "Legend of the Virgin and Her sleeveless Garment," by Chaucer's disciple Thomas Hoccleve. This text is found in the manuscript of the *Canterbury Tales* at Christ Church, Oxford, as well as in the holograph manuscript of Hoccleve's poems in the Huntington Library. The other Plowman's Tale is printed in William Thynne's edition of *The Workes of Geffray Chaucer*, published in 1542; it is also included by later editors as one of the Canterbury tales. John Urry's edition of 1721 even goes to the length of providing an engraving of the Plowman. Still more to be regretted is the absence of the Host's portrait from the Ellesmere Chaucer. Since the Host related no tale of his own, but merely

Upon this Somонд, and I biseche ye

But if I telle tales, two or thre

Of freres, er I come to Sidyngborne

That I shal make thyn herte for to morne

For wel I woot thy pacience is gon

Oure hoost gan pees, and that anon

And seyde, lat the womman telle hir tale

Ye fare as folk that dronken be of ale

Do, dame, telle forth youre tale, and that is best

Al redy, sir, quod she, right as yow lest

If I have licence of this worthy frere

Yis, dame, quod he, tel forth, and I wol heere

Heere endeth the Wyf of Bathe hir prologe, And
bigynneth hir tale

In tholde dayes of kyng Arthour,

Of which that Britons speken greet honour,

Al was this land fulfild of fayerye,

The elf queene, with hir ioly compaignye,

Daunced ful ofte in many a grene mede.

This was the olde opinion, as I rede.

I speke of manye hundred yeres ago.

But now kan no man se none elves mo,

For now the grete charitee and prayeres

Of lymytours and othere hooly freres,

That serchen every lond and every streem,

As thikke as motes in the sonne beem,

Blessynge halles, chambres, kichenes, boures,

Citees, burghes, castels, hye toures,

Thropes, bernes, shipnes, dayeryes,

This maketh that ther been no fayeryes.

For ther as wont to walken was an elf,

Ther walketh now the lymytour hym self,

In undermeles and in morwenynges,

And seyth his matyns and his hooly thynges

As he gooth in his lymytacioun.

Wommen may go saufly up and doun,

In every bussh or under every tree,

Ther is noon oother incubus but he,

And he ne wol doon hem but dishonour.

And so bifel that this kyng Arthour

Hadde in hous a lusty bacheler,

That on a day cam ridynge fro ryver,

And happed that, allone as he was born,

He saugh a mayde walkynge hym biforn,

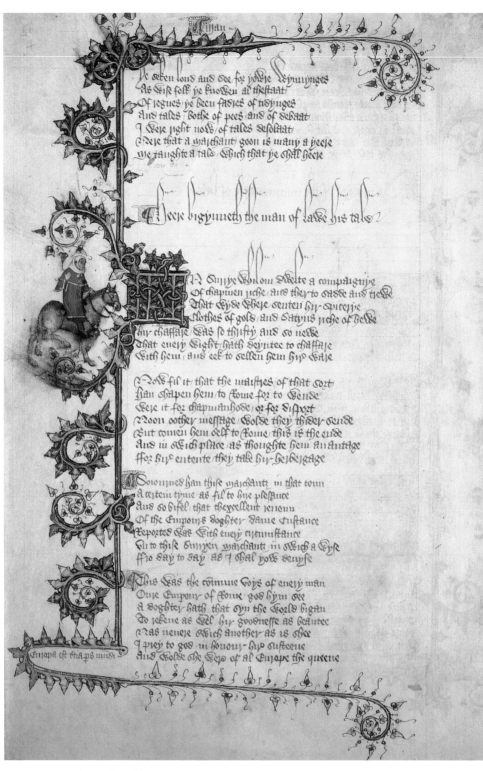

Titan

Ye seken lond and see for youre wynnynges
As wise folk ye knowen al thestaat
Of regnes ye been fadres of tydynges
And tales bothe of pees and of debaat
I were right now of tales desolaat
Nere that a marchaunt goon is many a yeere
Me taughte a tale which that ye shal heere

Heere bigynneth the man of lawe his tale

In Surrye whilom dwelte a compaignye
Of chapmen riche and therto sadde and trewe
That wyde where senten hir spicerye
Clothes of gold and satyns riche of hewe
Hir chaffare was so thrifty and so newe
That every wight hath deyntee to chaffare
With hem and eek to sellen hem hir ware

Now fil it that the maistres of that sort
Han shapen hem to Rome for to wende
Were it for chapmanhode or for disport
Noon oother message wolde they thider sende
But comen hem self to Rome this is the ende
And in which place as thoughte hem auantage
For hir entente they take hir herbergage

Soiourned han thise marchantz in that toun
A certein tyme as fil to hire plesaunce
And so bifel that thexcellent renoun
Of the Emperours doghter dame Custance
Reported was with euery circumstance
Vn to thise Surryen marchantz in which a wyse
I shal yow seyn as I shal yow deuyse

This was the commune voys of euery man
Oure Emperour of Rome god hym see
A doghter hath that syn the world bigan
To rekene as wel hir goodnesse as beautee
Nas neuere swich another as is shee
I prey to god in honour hir sustene
And wolde she were of al Europe the queene

Europa est quarta pars mundi

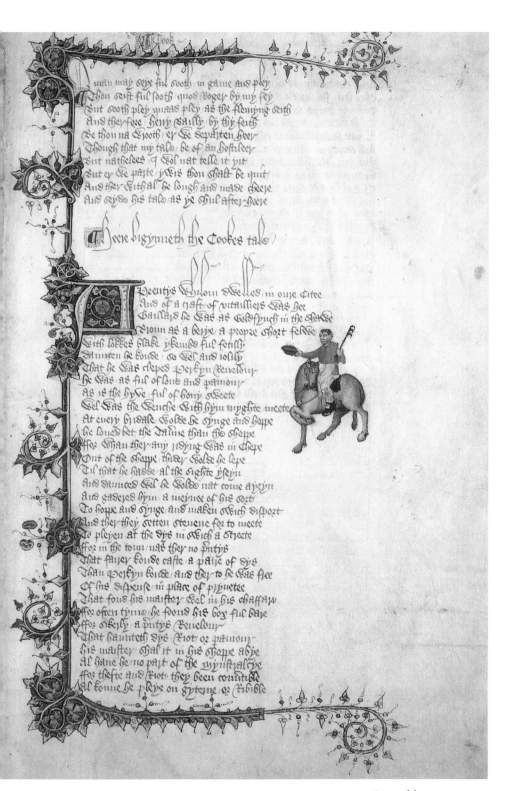

man may seye ful sooth in game and pley
Thou seist ful sooth quod Roger by my fey
But sooth pley quaas pley as the flemyng seith
And therfore Henry Bailly by thy feith
Be thou nat wrooth er we departen heer
Though that my tale be of an hostileer
But nathelees I wol nat telle it yit
But er we parte y-wis thou shalt be quit
And ther with al he lough and made cheere
And seyde his tale as ye shul after heere

Heere bigynneth the Cookes tale

A Prentys whilom dwelled in oure citee
And of a craft of vitailliers was hee
Gaillard he was as goldfynch in the shawe
Broun as a berye a propre short felawe
With lokkes blake y-kembd ful fetisly
Dauncen he koude so wel and iolily
That he was cleped Perkyn Revelour
He was as ful of love and paramour
As is the hyve ful of hony sweete
Wel was the wenche with hym myghte meete
At every brydale wolde he synge and hoppe
He loved bet the taverne than the shoppe
For whan ther any ridyng was in chepe
Out of the shoppe thider wolde he lepe
Til that he hadde al the sighte y-seyn
And daunced wel he kolde nat come ayeyn
And gadered hym a meynee of his sort
To hoppe and synge and maken swich disport
And ther they setten stevene for to meete
To pleyen at the dys in swich a streete
For in the toun nas ther no prentys
That fairer koude caste a paire of dys
Than Perkyn koude and ther to he was free
Of his dispense in place of pryvetee
That fond his maister wel in his chaffare
For often tyme he foond his box ful bare
For sikerly a prentys Revelour
That haunteth dys riot or paramour
His maister shal it in his shoppe abye
Al have he no part of the mynstralcye
For thefte and riot they been convertible
Al konne he pleye on gyterne or ribible

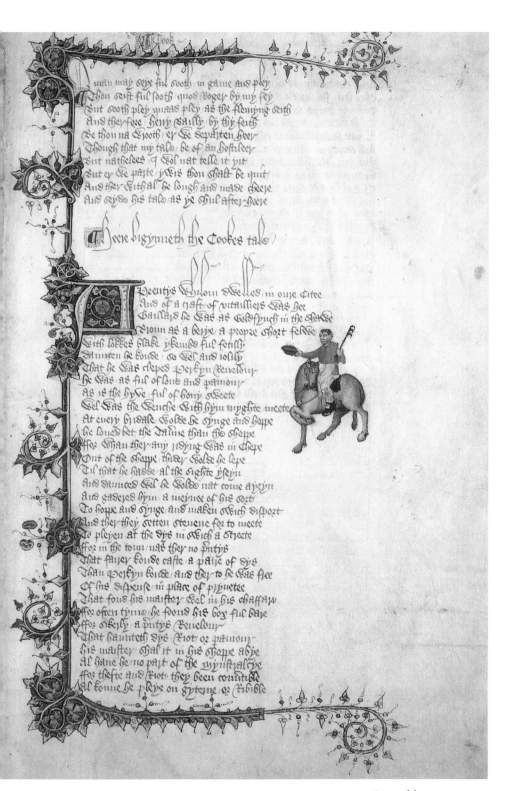

commented on those of the other Pilgrims, we must remain satisfied with the picture Chaucer conveys in words.

As long ago as 1870, the work of more than one artist in these paintings of the Pilgrims was detected by W. H. Hooper. This engraver cut the illustrations on wood for publication, in color, by the Chaucer Society. The result is a series of illustrations which are picturesque as woodcuts but inadequate to convey the details of the original to the modern critical scholar. Hooper called attention to the two groups, one with patches of grass under the horses' feet, the other without. The former he considered less good, with "colors badly ground and of poor quality." More recent studies have suggested three, or possibly four, different artists:

1. The portrait of Chaucer (4 inches in height, folio 153v).

2. The Monk, Nun's Priest, Second Nun, Canon's Yeoman, and Manciple ($2\frac{1}{4}$ to $3\frac{7}{8}$ inches, folios 169, 179, 187, 194, and 203, respectively).

3. The remaining paintings, which may be by a single artist, or by two working in similar styles ($1\frac{7}{8}$ to $2\frac{7}{8}$ inches; the Knight, $3\frac{3}{4}$).

Artists 1 and 2 place patches of grass beneath the horses' feet, but these are omitted by artist 3. The difference between the first two lies in the superior skill displayed in the Chaucer portrait, although the proportions of the figure are poor. This latter peculiarity could be explained by the use of a conventional portrait of Chaucer to provide the artist with an authentic likeness from which to copy the upper, more crucial part of the figure, and his then adapting the lower part to the riding position and to the limited space available in the margin of the leaf.

One of the most notable features of the paintings is the care exercised by the artists in following, as closely as conditions would permit, the descriptions of the Pilgrims given by Chaucer in his General Prologue. The Squire's enormously long sleeves flapping in the breeze and his immodestly short jacket in the latest fashionable cut are graphically shown. Of all the Pilgrims, he and the Merchant are the most elegantly dressed. While more conservative in style, as befits his station, the Merchant's "mottelee" gown has been pictured by the artist in a colorful pattern of blue and white flowers on a red ground. His "forked berd" is neatly trimmed, and his "Flaundrish bever hat" was doubtless an object of much pride and envy. Two greyhounds disporting themselves beside the Monk betray his love of "hunting for the hare" and his determination to "lat Austin have his swink to him reserved." The spurs worn by the buxom Wife of Bath seem not to be out of keeping with her particular antecedents, and the crepine under her "hat as brood as is a bokeler" frames a face still full of the youthful charm that had already ensnared five husbands. Even such a minutia as the Miller's gilded thumb was not overlooked by the artist, who may himself have learned from experience that the proverb "Honest millers have golden thumbs" was not without some foundation.

The same faithfulness to Chaucer's text is seen in the horses on which the Pilgrims ride. Chaucer's is quite the best-painted animal of the lot, and he walks at an appropriately measured pace upon a greensward dotted with red flowers. Whether by coincidence or intent, the artist provided a lively curvetting horse for each of the most stylish figures, the Squire and the Merchant, the one a "lusty bacheler," the other a disillusioned soul who laments that "We wedded men lyve in sorwe and care," each of them eager to change his state for that of the other. The dappled stallion of the Reeve and the lean horse of the poor but learned Clerk draw their characteristics from Chaucer's text.

Three of the paintings display a curious feature. In the figures of the Franklin, Shipman, and Squire, the horses have first been traced with a stylus from a medieval copybook, leaving a deep indentation in the vellum as an outline for the artist to follow.

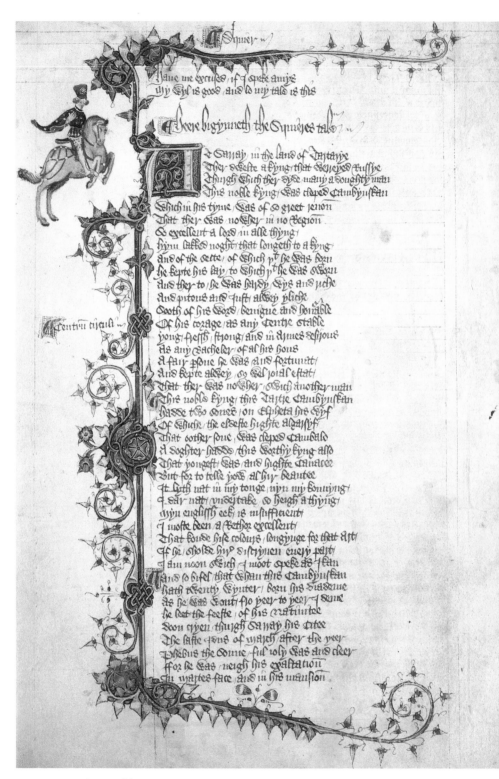

Have me excused / if I speke amys
My wyl is good / and lo my tale is this

Heere bigynneth the Squieres tale

At Sarray / in the land of Tartarye
Ther dwelte a kyng / that werreyed Russye
Thurgh which ther dyde many a doughty man
This noble kyng / was cleped Cambyuskan
Which in his tyme / was of so greet renoun
That ther was nowher / in no regioun
So excellent a lord in alle thyng
Hym lakked noght / that longeth to a kyng
And of the secte / of which þt he was born
He kepte his lay / to which þt he was sworn
And therto / he was hardy wys and riche
And pitous and iust / alwey yliche
Sooth of his word / benigne and honurable
Of his corage / as any centre stable
Yong fressh strong / and in armes desirous
As any bacheler / of al his hous
A fair persone he was and fortunat
And kepte alwey / so wel royal estat
That ther was nowher / swich another man
This noble kyng / this Tartre Cambyuskan
Hadde two sones / on Elpheta his wyf
Of whiche / the eldeste highte Algarsyf
That oother sone / was cleped Cambalo
A doghter hadde / this worthy kyng also
That yongest was / and highte Canacee
But for to telle yow / al hir beautee
It lyth nat in my tonge / nyn my konnyng
I dar nat vndertake / so heigh a thyng
Myn englyssh eek / is insufficient
I moste been / a rethor excellent
That koude hise coloures / longynge for that art
If he sholde hir / discryuen euery part
I am noon swich / I moot speke as I can
And so bifel that whan this Cambyuskan
Hath twenty wynter / born his diademe
As he was wont / fro yeer to yeer I deme
He leet the feeste / of his natiuitee
Doon cryen thurgh out / Sarray his citee
The laste ydus of March / after the yeer
Phebus the sonne / ful ioly was and cleer
For he was neigh his exaltacion
In Martes face / and in his mansion

THE SQUIRE, fol. 115v

The color was then applied and the rider placed in position in freehand. In the case of the Franklin, this tracing was impressed on the vellum with considerably more force than in the other two, and the indentation was transferred clearly onto the two preceding leaves but does not extend beyond them. Normally, this might have no significance, but, as it happens, the two preceding leaves are the first two leaves of the quire. This circumstance could be interpreted as evidence that the paintings were finished while the volume was in quires, before being bound—in short, that the paintings are contemporary rather than added at a later date as was at one time proposed.

Other clues pointing in the same general direction appear in the relationship between the marginal decoration, about which more will be said below, and the paintings of the Pilgrims. Apart from the Miller, none of the Pilgrims is painted on the inner margins of the leaves, a location deemed unsuitable for this kind of illustrative matter for a number of reasons. The width of this inner margin cannot be judged from the Manchester facsimile edition of the Ellesmere Chaucer, in which the margin was widened (while the outer margin was reduced, by way of compensation) to present a better appearance of the facsimile page. Wherever the beginning of a tale falls on the verso of a leaf, the illuminator appears to have intentionally reduced the amount of decoration alongside the opening four-line capital letter, an area he would otherwise have filled with sprays of leaves, flowers, or similar ornamentation. At the Miller's Tale no such space was left for the figure. The decorative border is so constructed at this point that any kind of erasure, made to allow space for the painting, would destroy the aesthetic effect. Since this is the first occurrence of a tale beginning on the verso of a leaf—the opening tale, by the Knight, having begun on a recto—it might be argued that the illuminator had not yet familiarized himself with all the details he was to take into consideration as his work proceeded. By the time the next such verso is reached, on which the Man of Law's Tale begins, a suitable niche has been left for the painting.

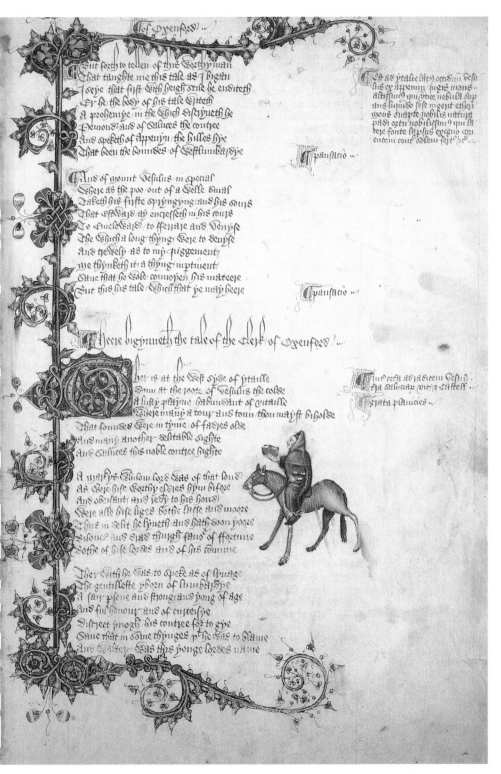

But forth to tellen of this worthy man
That taughte me this tale as I bigan
I seye that first with heigh stile he enditeth
Er he the body of his tale writeth
A prohemye in the which discryueth he
Pemond and of Saluces the contree
And speketh of Appenyn the hilles hye
That been the boundes of Westlumbardye

And of mount Vesulus in special
Where as the poo out of a welle smal
Taketh his firste spryngyng and his cours
That estward ay encresseth in his cours
To Emeleward to ffferare and Venyse
The which a long thyng were to deuyse
And trewely as to my iuggement
me thynketh it a thyng impertinent
Saue that he wole conueyen his mateere
But this his tale which that ye may heere

Heere bigynneth the tale of the Clerk of Oxenford

Ther is at the west syde of ytaille
Doun at the roote of Vesulus the colde
A lusty playne habundant of vitaille
Where many a tour and toun thou mayst biholde
That founded were in tyme of fadres olde
And many another delitable sighte
And Saluces this noble contree highte

A markys whilom lord was of that lond
As were hise worthy elders hym bifore
And obeisant and redy to his hond
Were alle hise liges bothe lasse and moore
Thus in delit he lyueth and hath doon yoore
Biloued and drad thurgh fauour of ffortune
Bothe of hise lordes and of his commune

Therwith he was to speke as of lynage
The gentilleste yborn of lumbardye
A fair persone and strong and yong of age
And ful of honour and of curteisye
Discreet ynogh his contree for to gye
Saue in somme thynges that he was to blame
And walter was this yonge lordes name

The most pronounced instance of the illuminator's adapting his border decoration to the anticipated requirements of the painting is offered by the Tale of Melibeus, which was to receive the most important portrait, that of Chaucer, against the opening lines of the text. An exceptionally large area was left free of decoration to take this finest of all the equestrian figures in the volume. In addition, the initial letter A, originally drawn in outline for the guidance of the illuminator, was moved slightly to the right when the gold and colors were applied, to allow even more adequate room for the horse's head to be inserted.

The five figures painted by artist 2 commence on the recto of folio 169 with that "fair prelat" the Monk and his two greyhounds coursing across the vellum page. He and the following four Pilgrims are all to be seen in the right outer margins on the rectos of the leaves, where the artist found ample space to treat his subjects in a very expansive manner. After these five Pilgrims have related their stories and posed for their likenesses, we come to the Parson, whose didactic and lengthy tale, if such it may be called, brings the volume to a close. In contrast to the preceding five tales, however, it begins on the verso of the leaf. The painting thus had to be fitted into a suitable niche among the embellishments of the decorative border, scarcely an ideal location for artist 2 with his unhampered style and generously proportioned figures. For this reason, perhaps, artist 3, who was accustomed to work with the more diminutive paintings—at least in the volume we are considering—was called upon to add the last of the Pilgrims. Apparently by inadvertence, the illuminator had placed a sprig of two pink-tipped daisy buds, similar to others on the same page, in the most appropriate spot for the figure. Being a very minor kind of hindrance, this was easily removed with a scraping knife and the painting of the Parson was then completed, altogether a fortunate turn of affairs, since the long lines of the prose text leave no space whatsoever on the inner margin for the painting.

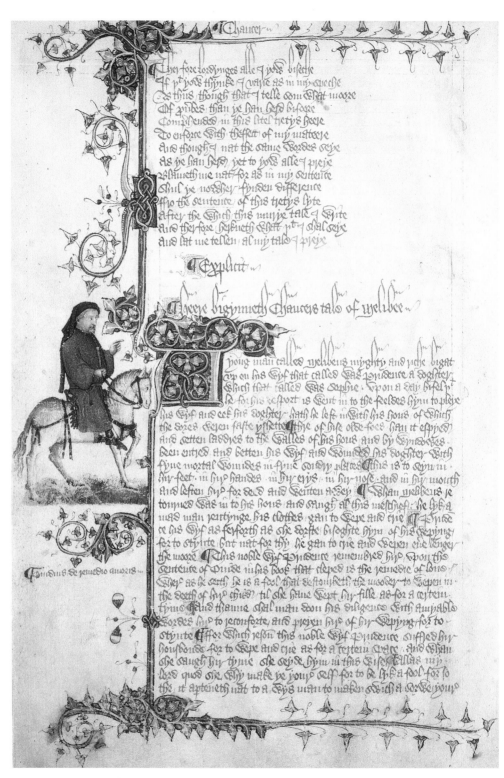

CHAUCER, fol. 153v

II. THE CHAUCER PORTRAIT

By far the most important of all these paintings is the portrait depicting Chaucer on horseback as he might have been seen riding to Canterbury in the company of the other Pilgrims whom he brought to life on his writing tablet. Other early portraits of Chaucer have also survived. In his poem *The Regiment of Princes* Thomas Hoccleve, who claims that Chaucer "fayn wold han me taght," mentions his master with much affection and refers to a painting in the margin of the manuscript intended "to putte other men in remembraunce" of his more celebrated mentor. Only three of the many manuscripts of the *Regiment* have this portrait of Chaucer. In most of them it was merely omitted, probably for lack of a competent artist or to avoid the added cost. However, one manuscript (British Museum, Harleian MS 4826) has had most of the painting cut away, which moved a sixteenth-century owner to relieve his indignation by writing these lines at the bottom of the page:

Off worthy Chaucer   Summe Furious Foole
here the pickture stood   Have Cutt the same in twayne
That much did wright   His deed doe shewe
and all to doe us good   He have a barren brayne

The relative merits of these early portraits have been studied in some detail, with the Ellesmere painting generally considered to be the best artistically. Its priority in date is supported by the later composition of the *Regiment* text during the period 1410–1412, a time at which the Ellesmere manuscript had undoubtedly been completed.

It will be recalled that when the time came for Chaucer to relate a tale for the entertainment of the other Pilgrims, he began with the story of Sir Thopas. The Host quickly grew weary of this "drasty speche" and interrupted Chaucer in the middle of a sentence with the words, "Namoore of this for goddes dignitee," whereupon Chaucer, after protesting the lack of appreciation for his story, began afresh with the Tale of Melibeus. It is curious to note that the portrait of Chaucer does not appear in the margin of the manuscript at the opening lines of Sir Thopas. Following the pattern established by the previous tales and repeated in all the others, the painting of the storyteller would normally be expected at this point. Its omission should serve to warn the reader—at least the reader who has the good fortune of consulting the original manuscript—that some further irregularity may lie immediately ahead, as to be sure it does. The beginning of Sir Thopas does not even enjoy the dignity of a decorative border; the opening lines of the text are marked only by a two-line initial, like hundreds of similar kind scattered throughout the volume.

Some careful consideration must have been given this problem by the medieval scribe, the illuminator, and perhaps the stationer in whose shop they may have worked, before their decision was reached. Should the Tale of Sir Thopas start off grandly amid a fanfare of gold and colors in the marginal decoration, further enhanced with a painting of Chaucer, only to disappoint the reader with an unfinished story? And then, having expended their chief effort on a false start, should they allow the complete Tale of Melibeus to commence less obtrusively and yet be the more important of the two? The absence of a border for Sir Thopas is obviously not due to a need for economy in the preparation of a volume that boasts seventy-one such handsomely decorated pages. It must point to a feeling on the part of all concerned— the scribe, the illuminator, the stationer—that a minimum of attention should be drawn to Sir Thopas, for the tale was destined to be a disappointment.

But this disappointment was only of a kind: the disappointment of an avid reader anticipating more of such pleasant tales as he had just been reading and suddenly finding his progress rudely halted by a loud "Namoore of this," well before he might have become certain of the author's real intention. Chaucer's point in writing the text of Sir Thopas as a literary and social satire was dramatically heightened by the uncontrollable outburst of the Host, and the early interruption of the tale permitted a suitable airing of the wearisome qualities satirized without the risk of losing a reader's patience in the process. In the interruption by the Host, Chaucer indicated the reaction he wanted to arouse in the other Pilgrims, with a shrewd eye carefully cocked at the reader. It would be interesting to know how seriously the artisans who prepared the Ellesmere Chaucer may have taken this aspect into consideration. Present-day attitudes might have favored a splendid opening page for Sir Thopas in the expectation that this would serve, by overemphasis, to heighten the ridiculous elements of the text which Chaucer took pains to weave into its fabric. The opening of Melibeus would then have been satisfactorily accommodated by a good decorative border and the reader would find himself none the worse off for the adventure. Could our present wishes have been foreseen, the problem might have been nicely solved by two portraits of Chaucer, one for Sir Thopas and one for Melibeus. Such an arrangement would have been quite justified, for Chaucer as a Pilgrim and teller of the story, and as author of all the Canterbury tales, plays a dual role. But it is not reasonable to expect that medieval scribes and artists should anticipate the interests of readers five hundred years hence.

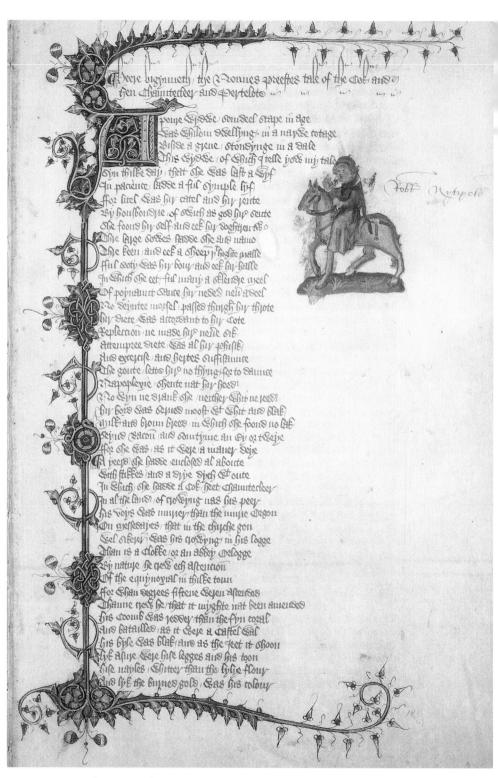

For it is ernest to me by my feith
That feele I wel what that any man seith
And yet for al my smert and al my grief
For al my sorwe labour and meschief
I koude nevere leve it in no wise
Now wolde god my wit myghte suffise
To tellen al that longeth to that art
And nathelees yow wol I tellen part
Syn that my lord is goon I wol nat spare
Swich thyng as that I knowe I wol declare

Heere endeth the prologe of the Chanouns yemannes tale

Heere bigynneth the Chanouns yeman his tale

With this Chanoun I dwelt have seven yeer
And of his science am I never the neer
Al that I hadde I have lost therby
And god woot so hath many mo than I
Ther I was wont to be right fressh and gay
Of clothyng and of oother good array
Now may I were an hose upon myn heed
And wher my colour was bothe fressh and reed
Now is it wan and of a leden hewe
Who so it useth soore shal he rewe
And of my swynk yet blered is myn eye
Lo which avantage is to multiplie
That slidynge science hath me maad so bare
That I have no good wher that evere I fare
And yet I am endetted so therby
Of gold that I have borwed trewely
That whil I lyve I shal it quite nevere
Lat every man be war by me for evere
What maner man that casteth hym therto
If he continue I holde his thrift ydo
For so helpe me god therby shal he nat wynne
But empte his purs and make his wittes thynne
And whan he thurgh his madnesse and folye
Hath lost his owene good thurgh jupartye
Thanne he excyteth oother folk therto
To lesen hir good as he hym self hath do
For unto shrewes joye it is and ese
To have hir felawes in peyne and disese
Thus was I ones lerned of a clerk
Of that no charge I wol speke of oure werk
Whan we been there as we shul exercise
Oure elvysshe craft we semen wonder wise

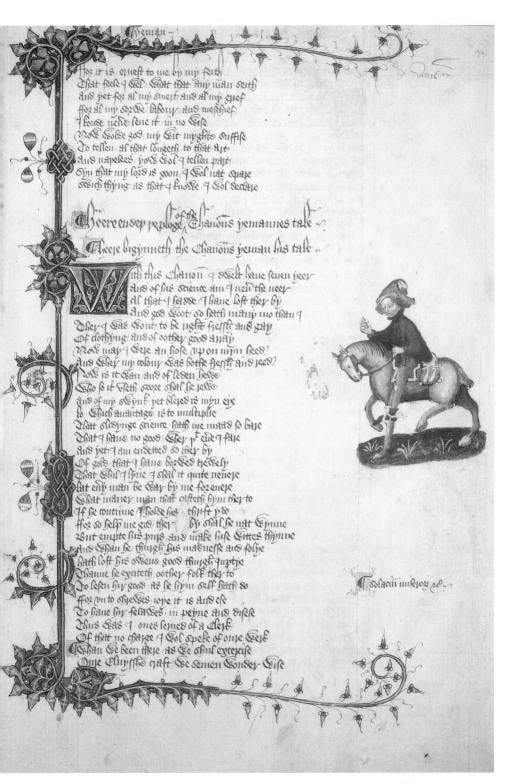

THE CANON'S YEOMAN, fol. 194r

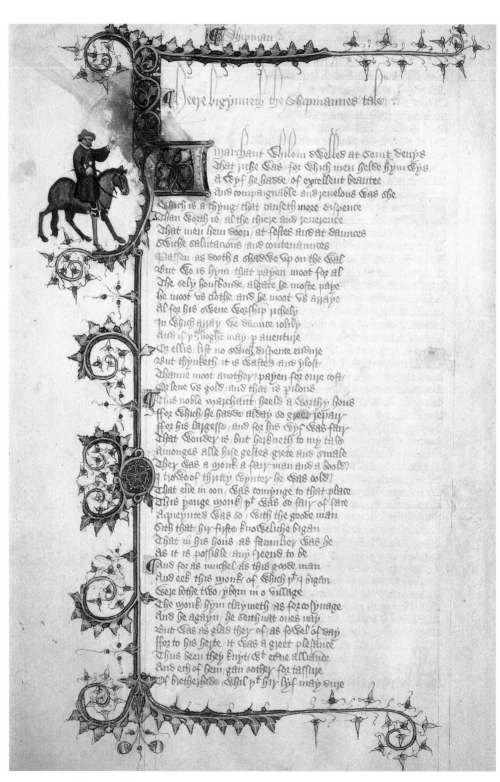

Prioress

Wherfore in laude, as I best kan or may,
Of thee, and of the whyte lylye flour
Which that the bar, and is a mayde alway,
To telle a storie I wol do my labour
Nat that I may encreessen hir honour
Ffor she hir self is honour and the roote
Of bountee next hir sone, and soules boote

O mooder mayde, o mayde mooder free
O bussh unbrent, brennynge in Moyses sighte,
That ravyshedest doun fro the deitee,
Thurgh thyn humblesse, the goost that in th'alighte,
Of whos vertu, whan he thyn herte lighte,
Conceyved was the fadres sapience,
Help me, to telle it in thy reverence

Lady, thy bountee, thy magnificence,
Thy vertu, and thy grete humylitee,
Ther may no tonge expresse, in no science
Ffor somtyme Lady, er men praye to thee,
Thou goost biforn, of thy benyngnytee
And getest us, thurgh lyght of thy preyere,
To gyden us, un to thy sone so deere

My konnyng is so wayk, o blisful queene
Ffor to declare thy grete worthynesse
That I no may, the weighte nat susteene
But as a child, of twelf monthe oold or lesse
That kan unnethe, any word expresse
Right so fare I, and therfore I yow preye
Gydeth my song, that I shal of yow seye

Explicit

Heere bigynneth the Prioresses tale

Ther was in Asye, in a greet citee
Amonges Cristene folk, a Jewerye
Sustened, by a lord of that contree
Ffor foul usure, and lucre of vileynye   The Sucum
Hateful to Crist, and to his compaignye
And thurgh this strete, men myghte ride or wende
Ffor it was free, and open at eyther ende

THE PRIORESS, fol. 148v

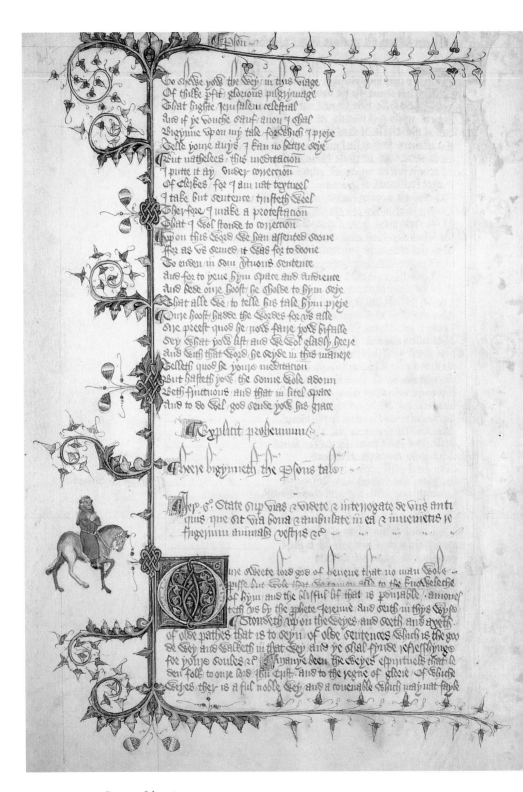

THE PARSON, fol. 206v

This nyght eo / as thise philosophres write
That heuene is swift and round and eek brennynge
Right eo was fayr Cecilie the white
ful swift and bisy eud in good wyrkynge
And round and hool in good perseuynge
And brennynge eud in charite ful brighte
Now haue I yow declared what she highte

❡ Explicit

❡ Heere bigynneth the Secounde Nonnes tale of the lyf
of Seinte Cecile

This mayden bright Cecilie as hir lif seith
Was comen of Romayns and of noble kynde
And from hir cradel vp fostred in the feith
Of Crist and bar his gospel in hir mynde
She neuere cessed as I writen fynde
Of hir preyere and god to loue and drede
Bisekynge hym to kepe hir maydenhede

And whan this mayden sholde vnto a man
Ywedded be / that was ful yong of age
Which that ycleped was Valerian
And day was comen of hir mariage
She ful deuout and humble in hir corage
Vnder hir robe of gold that sat ful faire
Hadde next hir flessh yclad hir in an haire

And whil the Orgues maden melodie
To god allone in herte thus sang she
O lord my soule and eek my body gye
Vnwemmed lest that it confounded be
And for his loue that dide vpon a tree
Euery seconde and thridde day she faste
Ay biddynge in hir orisons ful faste

The nyght cam and to bedde moste she gon
With hir housbonde as ofte is the manere
And pryuely to hym she seyde anon
O swete and wel biloued spouse deere
Ther is a conseil and ye wolde it heere
Which that right fayn I wolde vnto yow seye
So that ye swere ye shul me nat biwreye

The three pages of Sir Thopas offer some measure of comfort to any admirer of the old-fashioned romances who may feel more provoked at the interruption than amused at the skillful parody. But this is possible only if he can see the manuscript, where the tail-rhyme stanzas are written in a complicated form with the third and sixth lines of each stanza—the "tails"—in a separate column and all rhymed line endings connected by pen strokes to create an exceptionally attractive appearance. It is unfortunate that many such nuances of early manuscripts are lost in transferring the text to a printed page.

iii. the Illumination

Quite apart from the paintings of the Pilgrims, the Ellesmere Chaucer is the most elaborately decorated of all the manuscripts of the *Canterbury Tales*. This is manifested in the exceptionally lavish use of three-quarter borders, or demi-vinets, as they were called by the medieval artists, on no fewer than seventy-one pages of the manuscript. These borders fill the left margin of the page and taper off horizontally into the upper and lower margins, leaving the right margin blank. They are usually made up of gold and colored bar-work extending vertically, with occasional interlacing, from which extend sprays and branches with trefoil-like leaves, daisy buds, and similar flower forms. All this was first sketched in outline on the page before the gold leaf and colors were applied. These borders are supplemented by about 225 large initials, or champs, in gold and colors, which vary from two to six lines in height, depending on the nature of the text they introduce. Lastly, there is a prodigal display of paragraph marks, also in gold and colors, with red or violet pen ornamentation, far too numerous to be counted—one page of the Parson's Tale alone having over forty such spots of color and brilliance to enliven the appearance of a solid page of text. All this extravagance combines to make the Ellesmere Chaucer one of the most handsome Middle English manuscripts to have survived from the period. Adding to its impressiveness is the stately size of the

Whiche that he it on / than he sholde with me stryue
¶ I wol nat wratthen hym also moot I thryue
That that I spak I seyde it in my bourde
And wite ye what I haue heer in a gourde
A draghte of wyn ye of a rype grape
And right anon ye shul seen a good jape
This Cook shal drynke ther of if pt I may
Vp peyne of deeth he wol nat seye me nay
¶ And certeynly to tellen as it was
Of this vessel the Cook drank faste allas
What nedes hym he drank ynough biforn
And whan he hadde pouped in this horn
To the Manciple he took the gourde agayn
And of that drynke the Cook was wonder fayn
And thanked hym in swich wise as he koude
¶ Thanne gan oure hoost to laughen wonder loude
And seyde I se wel it is necessarie
Where pt we goon pt drynke we wt vs carie
ffor that wol turne rancour and disese
Tacord and loue and many a wrong apese
¶ O Bacus yblessed be thy name
That so kanst turnen ernest in to game
Worshipe and thank be to thy deitee
Of that mateere ye gete namoore of me
Telle on thy tale Manciple I thee preye
¶ Wel sire quod he now herkneth what I seye

Heere bigynneth the manciples tale of the Crowe

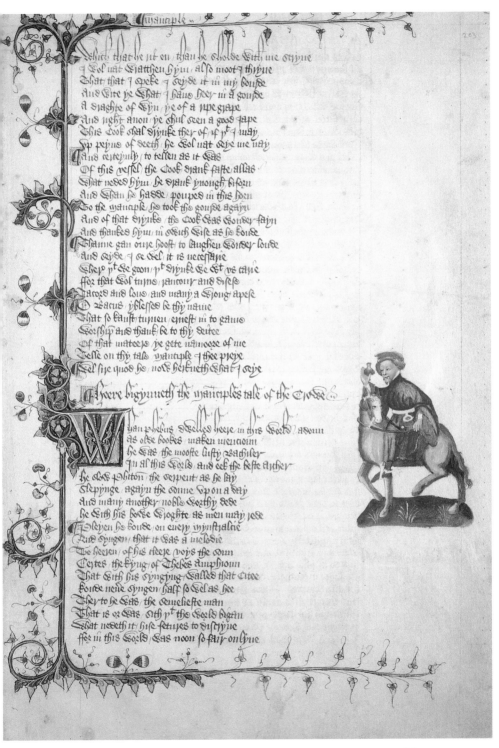

W
han Phebus dwelles heere in this world adoun
As olde bookes maken mencioun
He was the mooste lusty bachiler
In al this world and eek the beste Archer
he slow Phitton the serpent as he lay
Slepynge agayn the sonne vpon a day
And many another noble worthy dede
he with his bowe wroghte as men may rede
¶ Pleyen he koude on euery mynstralcie
And syngen that it was a melodie
To heeren of his clere voys the soun
Certes the kyng of Thebes Amphioun
That with his syngyng walled that citee
Koude neuere syngen half so wel as hee
Therto he was the semelieste man
That is or was sith pt the world bigan
What nedeth it hise fetures to discryue
ffor in this world was noon so fair onlyue

THE MANCIPLE, fol. 203r

¶ The prologe of the marchantes tale

Wepyng and waylyng, care and oother sorwe
I knowe ynogh, on even and a-morwe,
Quod the marchaunt, and so doon oothere mo
That wedded been, I trowe that it be so
For wel I woot, it fareth so with me
I have a wyf, the worste that may be
For thogh the feend to hir ycoupled were
She wolde hym overmacche, I day wel swere
What sholde I yow reherce in special
Hir hye malice, she is a shrewe at al
Ther is a long and large difference
Bitwix Grisildis grete pacience.
And of my wyf the passyng crueltee
Were I unbounden, also moot I thee
I wolde nevere eft, comen in the snare
We wedded men lyven in sorwe and care
Assaye whoso wole, and he shal fynde
That I seye sooth, by Seint Thomas of Inde
As for the moore part, I sey nat alle
God shilde that it sholde so bifalle
A, goode sire Hoost, I have ywedded bee
Thise monthes two, and moore nat, pardee
And yet, I trowe, he that al his lyve
Wyflees hath been, though that men wolde him ryve
Unto the herte, ne koude in no manere
Tellen so muchel sorwe as I now heere
Koude tellen, of my wyves cursednesse
Now, quod oure Hoost, marchant, so god yow blesse
Syn ye so muchel knowen of that art
Ful hertely I pray yow telle us part
Gladly, quod he, but of myn owene soore
For soory herte, I telle may namoore

¶ Heere bigynneth the marchantes tale

Whilom ther was dwellynge in Lumbardye
A worthy knyght, that born was of Pavye
In which he lyved in greet prosperitee
And sixty yeer a wyflees man was hee
And folwed ay his bodily delyt
On wommen, ther as was his appetyt

THE MERCHANT, fol. 102v

volume, its height of 15¾ inches and its width of 11⅛ inches placing it among the largest of the extant manuscripts of the *Tales*.

As we have already seen, the illuminator disappointed us in omitting his customary border for the Tale of Sir Thopas. Before completing his work on the manuscript, he again surprises us, but now with a quite dazzling profusion of decorative borders for the concluding Parson's Tale. The structure of this so-called tale, a sermon on penitence in three parts which embodies a discussion of the seven mortal sins along with remedies for each, offers numerous opportunities for a border at the opening of each section. No fewer than fifteen such decorative borders, or slightly under a fourth of the total number for the entire volume, are crowded into the last twenty-seven leaves of the volume. If the text of the Parson's Tale strikes the modern reader as rather wearisome, it is no fault of the illuminator, whose efforts make many of the pages sparkle with gold and colors.

The illumination of the volume bears a much closer relationship to the conservative tradition of the late fourteenth century than to the new style which developed in England a few years later. This may be seen from its similarity to a Missal made for Abbot Nicholas Lytlington, at Westminster, in 1383–1384 (now in the Westminster Abbey Library), and the much stronger resemblance to a Psalter begun for Simon Montacute, Bishop of Ely (d. 1345), and completed later in the fourteenth century for use in the Ely diocese (deposited in the British Museum in 1936). It is recognized that medieval English manuscripts in the vernacular are not notable as a class (in contrast to such a group as the Books of Hours) for the excellence and elaborateness of their decoration. One reason for this can possibly be the trilingual structure of languages in England brought about by the Norman Conquest—Latin for the clergy, French for the ruling classes, with English relegated to the ubiquitous "common man." The resulting disfavor into which the native tongue fell persisted for many generations. By Chaucer's lifetime an expanding use of English was already under way, gaining momentum as the

fifteenth century progressed. The result was an increasing
demand for texts in English—whether of a literary or factual
nature—from the new reading public. But this demand was not
at first supported by a wealth that could command the luxury of
beautifully illuminated manuscripts at will, nor was the prestige
of the English language itself sufficiently advanced to justify a lavish form of text decoration as a general procedure. Consequently
the stationer would be compelled to minimize his dependence on
artists and illuminators in the preparation of English manuscripts
and would call upon their serious efforts only when a specially
commissioned volume was planned for some person of wealth
and importance. Such a volume was the Ellesmere Chaucer; and
that its entertaining English text should also be amply endowed
with diverse features which made heavy demands on the talents
of both illuminators and artists can only be explained by some
very special circumstances in its preparation. Just what these circumstances were or who may have been the persons involved we
do not know, but some possibilities will be proposed later on.

IV. THE TEXT

AT ONE TIME the Ellesmere Chaucer was thought to preserve the most satisfactory text to be found in any of the *Canterbury Tales* manuscripts. As more detailed comparative studies were made by scholars, that opinion was modified somewhat. However, the number of its excellent readings, whether unique or shared by another manuscript, places it easily among the best that are available. For this reason it was chosen, along with the Hengwrt manuscript (in the National Library of Wales), which may even have been written by the same scribe, as the basic text for John M. Manly's and Edith Rickert's definitive eight-volume edition of the *Canterbury Tales*.

The Ellesmere text gives every indication of having been edited by some very intelligent person, a task made necessary by Chaucer's apparent failure to complete the work, even in abbreviated form. While no manuscript of the tales dating from his lifetime has survived to the present, one or two of the individual stories are known to have been read by, and were probably owned by, some of his contemporaries. Others, whether complete or fragmentary, were undoubtedly among his possessions at the time of his death in 1400. The incomplete state of the two fragmentary tales, those of the Cook and the Squire, caused the Ellesmere scribe to leave space for the missing text, in the hope that it might still be inserted when discovered. It is worth noting that the Hengwrt scribe also left space for the missing text, but

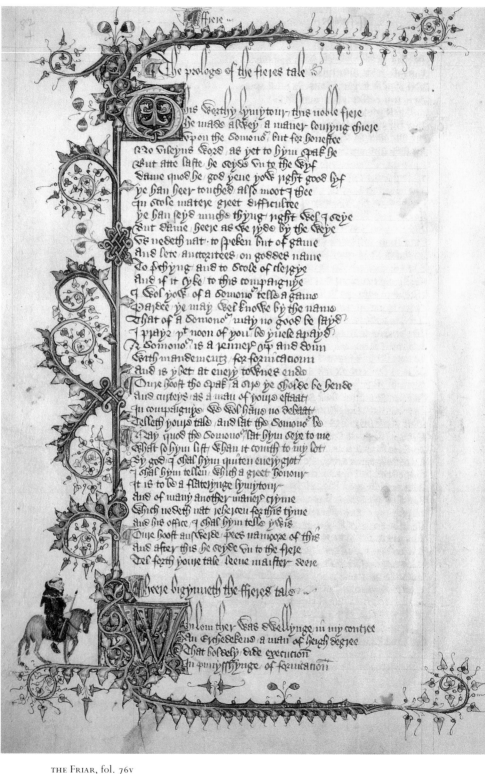

The prologe of the freres tale

This worthy lymytour this noble frere
He made alwey a maner louryng cheere
Upon the somonour but for honestee
No vileyns word as yet to hym spak he
But atte laste he seyde vn to the wyf
Dame quod he god yeue yow right good lyf
Ye han heer touched also moot I thee
In scole matere greet difficultee
Ye han seyd muche thyng right wel I seye
But dame heere as we ryde by the weye
Us nedeth nat to speken but of game
And lete auctoritees on goddes name
To prechyng and to scole of clergye
And if it lyke to this compaignye
I wol yow of a somonour telle a game
Pardee ye may wel knowe by the name
That of a somonour may no good be sayd
I praye that noon of you be yuele apayd
A somonour is a rennere vp and doun
With mandementz for fornicacioun
And is ybet at euery townes ende
Oure hoost tho spak a nay ye sholde be hende
And curteys as a man of youre estaat
In compaignye we wol haue no debaat
Telleth youre tale and lat tho somonour be
Nay quod the somonour lat hym seye to me
What so hym list whan it comth to my lot
By god I shal hym quiten euerygrot
I shal hym tellen which a greet honour
It is to be a flaterynge lymytour
And of many another manere cryme
Which nedeth nat rehercen for this tyme
And his office I shal hym telle ywis
Oure hoost answerde pees namoore of this
And after this he seyde vn to the frere
Tel forth youre tale leeue maister deere

Heere bigynneth the freres tale

Whilom ther was dwellynge in my contree
An erchedeken a man of heigh degree
That boldely dide execucioun
In punysshynge of fornicacioun

THE FRIAR, fol. 76v

after coming to the conclusion that it had never been written he added the comment, "Of this Cokes tale maked Chaucer na moore." No such comment appears in the somewhat later Ellesmere manuscript at this point, although both volumes appear to have been written by one and the same person. These and numerous similar problems compelled the earliest scribes to become editors of this literary legacy despite themselves, and the varying success of their efforts has provided present-day students with ample grist for the mills of Chaucerian scholarship.

Another important asset of the Ellesmere Chaucer is the completeness of its text. To some this may not appear unusual, or more than what should normally be expected, but the fact that only fourteen of the eighty-two manuscripts of the *Canterbury Tales* preserve the text unmutilated proves that completeness is not as common a virtue as would be desirable. It is not exceptional for a medieval manuscript to have lost a leaf or two, occasionally even a quire at the beginning or end in the course of its migration through the centuries. How much greater, then, is the chance of loss when the volume is embellished with eye-catching decorative borders in gold and colors, to say nothing of charming little equestrian paintings in the margin which can readily excite the covetousness of a viewer. Through such a long period as five hundred years, only a few moments' neglect of careful supervision, when occurring under the evil conjunction of a sharp knife and irresistible temptation, can result in the mutilation of an originally fine manuscript.

A volume of the *Canterbury Tales* now preserved in the Cambridge University Library (MS.Gg.4.27) regretfully exemplifies this kind of unfortunate accident all too vividly, for it, like the Ellesmere Chaucer, had once been illustrated with paintings of all the Pilgrims, but only six now remain. The rest, including a few pages with attractive borders, have fallen prey to the vandalism of some misguided person. It would have been a serious enough business had these excised leaves luckily survived elsewhere, but when the act of mutilation is also the cause of their destruction,

Of oother folk / he saugh ynowe in wo
Vn to this Angel / spak the frere tho
Now sir quod he / han freres swich a grace
That noon of hem / shal come to this place?
Yis quod this Angel / many a millioun
And vn to Sathanas / he ladde hym doun
And now hath Sathanas / seith he a tayl
Bredder than of a Carryk / is the sayl
Hoold vp thy tayl thou Sathanas quod he
Shewe forth thyn ers / and lat the frere se
Where is the nest of freres / in this place
And er pt half a furlong wey of space
Right so as bees / out swarmen from an hyue
Out of the deueles ers / they gonne dryue
Twenty thousand freres / in a route
And thurgh out helle / swarmeden aboute
And comen agayn / as faste as they may gon
And in his ers / they crepten euerychon
He clapte his tayl agayn / and lay ful stille
This frere Whan he hadde looked al his fille
Vpon the tormentz / of this sory place
His spirit god restored / of his grace
Vn to his body agayn / and he awook
But nathelees for fere / yet he quook
So was the deueles ers / ay in his mynde
That is his heritage / of verray kynde
God saue yow alle / saue this cursed frere
My prologe wol I ende / in this manere

Heere bigynneth the Somonos his tale

A lepers ther is in yorkshire / as I gesse
A mersshcountree / called holdernesse
In which ther wente a lymytour aboute
To preche / and eek to begge / it is no doute
And so bifel / that on a day this frere
Hadde preched at a chirche / in his manere
And specially / abouen euery thyng
Excited he the peple / in his prechyng
To trentals / and to yeue for goddes sake
Wher with men myghte hooly houses make
Ther as diuine seruyce / is honoured
Nat ther / it wasted is and deuoured
Ne ther / it nedeth nat for to be yeue
As to possessioners / that mowen lyue

our loss is sadly an irreparable one and all the more grievous since another early portrait of Chaucer was undoubtedly included among them. Again, in the manuscript designated as "Oxford" (see Bibliographical Notes), we find that only thirteen leaves, three of them with paintings of Pilgrims, have survived from a volume that probably contained the entire series when in its complete state. Obviously it was the attractiveness of the paintings themselves which brought about their almost complete destruction in these two manuscripts. In view of their unhappy fate, it is all the more fortunate that the Ellesmere Chaucer, with its even more authentic series, should have escaped similar disfigurement. The picture gallery of twenty-three Canterbury Pilgrims it has thus preserved for the enlightenment and pleasure of later generations is a unique graphic heritage from medieval times.

Since we have referred briefly to the two other series of illustrations, a few words of comment on their comparative quality should be added. In the opinion of Roger S. Loomis, *A Mirror of Chaucer's World* (1965), the artists of these two manuscripts completely disregard Chaucer's descriptions of the Pilgrims. He concludes, "Far superior as illustration of Chaucer's text is the complete set of miniatures of the tellers of the tales in the Ellesmere manuscript."

Another aspect of the volume's completeness, quite apart from any reference to deliberate excisions perpetrated at a later date, is the presence of as full a text as the editors had been able to salvage from Chaucer's effects and from manuscripts already in circulation. The Ellesmere manuscript is more complete than any other of equal accuracy, and it is more accurate than any other of similar completeness. On this score alone, then, the Ellesmere Chaucer becomes the one manuscript which, independent of all others, provides us with the most superior text of the *Canterbury Tales*.

v. the History of the Manuscript

THE HISTORY of the Ellesmere Chaucer over the past five hundred years is not out of character with the other noteworthy aspects of the volume. Direct evidence concerning the persons for whom the manuscript was made is lacking, but some speculation on the identity of other early owners should not be omitted. One possibility is suggested by the poem on flyleaves 2 to 4, written as a tribute to the De Vere family, earls of Oxford. John de Vere, twelfth Earl of Oxford, born in 1408, could not have been the original owner, but he was brought into contact with men interested in books at an early age. After his father's death in 1417, he became the ward of the Duke of Exeter and in 1426 of the Duke of Bedford. The latter's fondness for fine manuscripts establishes him as one of the most prominent manuscript collectors of the fifteenth century. Both of these men were kinsmen of Chaucer's son Thomas, who may reasonably be supposed to have been closely interested in the preparation of a "definitive" edition of the *Tales*, such as the Ellesmere Chaucer was intended to be. The strong similarity of its illumination to that in the Lytlington Missal, previously mentioned, could have resulted from Thomas Chaucer's association with Westminster and a desire to see the volume decorated in the same handsome style and perhaps even by the same artists.

If the manuscript had been in the possession of the twelfth Earl of Oxford, it could then have come by inheritance to his

son John, thirteenth Earl of Oxford, Hereditary Lord Great
Chamberlain of England and holder of many other important
offices of state. It is of some significance in displaying the background of family interest in literary affairs to know that the latter
was a patron of William Caxton and that his mother, Elizabeth,
Countess of Oxford, had also been a patron of literature; at her
request Osbern Bokenham made his translation of the "Lyf of S.
Elyzabeth." On the death, in 1513, of the thirteenth earl, who left
no descendants, an inventory of his property was drawn up
which included "A Chest full of frenshe and englisshe bokes." We
must submit ourselves to the exasperation of having no itemized
list of these "englisshe bokes." Among the legatees of the earl's
will were his ward, Sir Giles Alington (a name we shall soon
encounter again), and George Waldegrave. Both of these persons
were sons-in-law of one of the executors of this same will: Sir
Robert Drury, of Hawsted, in Suffolk, just seventeen miles
northeast of Castle Hedingham, the family seat of the De Veres.

Sir Robert Drury was speaker of the House of Commons
in 1495 and a member of Henry VIII's Council. By his father's will
he had received some "bocks of Latyn," while his brother, William,
was bequeathed "ij Inglyshe books called Bochas of Lydgat's making." Sir Robert died in 1536, but his will has disappeared and
so we have no further clues to the contents or disposition of his
library. On the first flyleaf of the Ellesmere Chaucer occur the
names of this Sir Robert Drury, of his sons, William and Robert,
and of his daughters, Anna, Bridget, and Ursula. Also on the same
page is written the name of Edward Waldegrave.

A slightly later inscription on folio 130, "per me Henricum
Payne," undoubtedly refers to Henry Payne, of Nowton, near
Hawsted, a wealthy lawyer and member of Lincoln's Inn, who
died in 1568. He was on friendly terms with the Drurys, had
been a witness to Sir William Drury's will in 1557, and had
inherited certain properties from him. Among the legatees of
Payne's will was Sir Giles Alington, grandson of the above-men-
tioned Ursula Drury Alington, to whom Payne bequeathed "my

Chaucer written on vellum and illumyned w^t golde." This is the first reference from sources outside the manuscript itself relating to ownership of the Ellesmere Chaucer.

Also on the flyleaves are some inscriptions by Roger, Lord North, Treasurer of the Royal Household, who was Sir Giles Alington's neighbor. Both men were visited by Queen Elizabeth on her royal progress through Norfolk in 1578. As a bibliophile, Lord North must have been deeply impressed by the magnifi-cence of his neighbor's Chaucer, and he probably had little peace of mind until he was able to write "Durum pati" on its flyleaves, a motto he frequently inscribed in the books he collected.

The manuscript must soon thereafter have passed into the Egerton family, earls of Bridgewater, for a pressmark in the hand-writing of the first earl (d. 1649) is found on a flyleaf at the be-ginning of the volume. The father of the first earl was Sir Thomas Egerton, Baron Ellesmere and Viscount Brackley, Keeper of the Great Seal under Queen Elizabeth, a royal servant like Lord North and, like him, also a member of the Privy Council. Sir Thomas was the founder of the Bridgewater Library, which is described by Seymour de Ricci, in his *English Collectors of Books and Manuscripts*, as probably "the oldest large family library in the United Kingdom." In 1604, Sir Thomas acquired Ashridge, in Hertfordshire, formerly the medieval monastic foundation known as the College of Bonshommes, and it was there that his library was installed and remained from one generation of the family to the next until the time of Francis, seventh Earl and third Duke of Bridgewater (1736–1803).

For the past three centuries the Ellesmere Chaucer has been spared the dangers which so often accompany continual change of ownership, but a closer acquaintance with one or two of those who inherited the Bridgewater Library during this time reveals unexpected hazards even under such apparently favorable condi-tions. One of the most critical periods was the lifetime of this same third duke, the famous canal builder and a shrewd man of business. Possessed of vast wealth at the time of his death, he had at one time found it necessary to dismiss all his servants but two or three and to board up the windows of Bridgewater House, in London, in order to conserve funds for the construction of his Manchester-Liverpool canal. Isaac Disraeli, in his *Curiosities of Literature*, describes one of the duke's less commendable projects: "The late Duke of Bridgewater, I am informed, burnt many of the numerous family papers, and bricked up a quantity, which, when opened after his death, were found to have perished. It is said he declared that he did not choose that his ancestors should be traced back to a person of mean trade, which it seems might possibly have been the case. The loss cannot now be appreciated; but unquestionably stores of history, and perhaps of literature, were sacrificed."

Contrary to previous indications, in later life the duke became an active and surprisingly astute collector of paintings, and it was probably a function of this innate faculty that permitted him to recognize the beauty and value of the Ellesmere Chaucer. Moreover, the manuscript was patently incapable of exposing family skeletons. In any case, it was spared a fate similar to that of the unfortunate Fortunato in Poe's grisly masterpiece, *The Cask of Amontillado*. More than twelve thousand manuscripts have survived in the Ellesmere Papers to bear testimony that the destruction mentioned by Disraeli was by no means carried out in a wholesale manner. This sacrifice to propriety by the third duke was ironically without the desired effect, for it is well known through other channels that the founder of the family fortunes, Sir Thomas Egerton, was the illegitimate son of a Cheshire village domestic servant. That he should have achieved such heights of prominence despite so inauspicious an origin, and thereby acquired a relatively greater personal stature, probably represented too democratic a point of view to have been entertained by the duke.

The third duke died unmarried in 1803, whereupon his extensive properties were distributed in accordance with the terms of a sixty-six-page will. His successor to the earldom of Bridgewater, John Egerton, a cousin, inherited Ashridge. The books, manuscripts, and paintings which had been housed there were bequeathed to the duke's nephew, George Leveson-Gower, second Marquess of Stafford, along with other estates, including Bridgewater House, London, the family's townhouse purchased by John, third Earl of Bridgewater, in about 1700. As a result of this division, the future home of the Ellesmere Chaucer became Bridgewater House instead of Ashridge. During this period, from 1803 to 1833, the manuscripts were usually referred to as the Stafford manuscripts, and the volume later to become known as the Ellesmere Chaucer was for thirty years the Stafford Chaucer. Upon the death of the Marquess of Stafford in 1833, the manuscripts descended to Francis, his second son and an Egerton through his paternal grandmother. He took the name of Egerton in lieu of Leveson-Gower and was created Earl of Ellesmere in 1846. His descendants continued in possession of the Bridgewater House Library until the first World War, when the burdensome taxes occasioned by the death of Francis, third Earl of Ellesmere in 1914, caused the books and manuscripts to be offered for sale by Sotheby & Co. in a special catalog issued during December 1916. The first lot, the pearl of the collection, was "The Ellesmere Chaucer."

In 1917, Henry E. Huntington acquired the entire Bridgewater Library en bloc. Ever since the Huntington Library was opened to the public in 1928, the Ellesmere Chaucer has been on exhibition in the appropriate company of such other bibliographical rarities as the most famous of all printed books, the Gutenberg Bible, the holograph autobiography of Benjamin Franklin begun while he was in England in 1771, and the stately eleventh-century Bible associated with the name of Bishop Gundulf, architect of the Tower of London. During this time several million persons have visited the Library exhibition halls and have had the opportunity of seeing the Chaucer manuscript on display. Their admiration for the beautifully illuminated volume inevitably leads to a deeper appreciation for the country of its origin. Chaucer astride his horse in the margin of the manuscript continues to be the ambassador of goodwill he undoubtedly was in life, but now at a distance of seven thousand miles in space and a span of six centuries in time. England could not easily find a better, then or now.

Bibliographical Description of the Manuscript

THE MANUSCRIPT is written on 232 vellum leaves of relatively good quality for English material of the period, measuring 15¾ × 11⅛ inches. The writing space is 12⅜ × 6⅛ inches, ruled with light-reddish ink in single columns for 48 lines of text. Four contemporary ruled flyleaves are placed at the beginning of the volume and four at the end. There are 29 quires of text, in eights, but all signature marks and catchwords have been trimmed away by the binder. The tops of only one group of catchwords have survived, at the end of quire 23, suggesting that at least an inch of vellum has been cut away at the bottom—perhaps more, if the scribe observed the customary proportions with the largest margin at the bottom. Since a number of the topmost ornaments are also cropped, at least another inch of vellum must have been lost there. Because of the presence of many marginal glosses, written by the original scribe, and also of the paintings of the Pilgrims, very little vellum has been removed from the fore edge. Most of the line prickings therefore remain intact, and from these it can be determined that the prickings were made through all eight leaves of each quire in one operation, from the first leaf to the last. . . .

One peculiarity of the vellum apparently not observed heretofore deserves mention in a manuscript of such importance, where every divergence from the normal requires investigation.

In each vellum leaf of the text throughout the volume, a horizontal crease may be seen, located at a distance of about four-and-a-half inches from the bottom edge. This crease was undoubtedly in the vellum before the writing and decoration were added. No obvious purpose is served by such creases, and we must conclude that some adventitious factor is involved. . . . It can be assumed that skins of vellum prepared by the medieval parchmenter for use by scribes were stored in his warehouse, like stocks of paper at a later date, awaiting a demand, and that the skins had been folded for ease of handling and storage. Thus large skins measuring about 24 × 36 inches, which is close to the maximum size carried by parchmenters in England at the present time, could originally have been folded twice to a 24 × 12-inch size for storage. This 12-inch height would be suitable for the average folio volume of the period. When the request came for the Chaucer manuscript and the parchmenter was unable at the moment to supply vellum sheets of the exceptionally large size required, he could have drawn on his stock of already folded skins. Measuring 24 × 36 inches in overall size when unfolded, they could have been flattened and then cut to 24 × 18 inches for the scribe's use, still retaining a slight crease from the previous fold.

Turning now to the measurements of the leaves in the Ellesmere Chaucer, if the several inches trimmed away at top and bottom by the binder are added to the manuscript's present 15¼-inch height, we would have a leaf of about 18 inches, corresponding closely to the height of the parchmenter's converted stock sheet just described. And the crease in the vellum where it is now just visible underneath the lines of text also corresponds to the crease in these converted sheets. The manuscript's present 11⅛-inch width is also in conformity with the 24-inch width of the blank sheet, which, when folded down the middle, would supply two leaves 12 inches in width. By some explanation such as this, the mystery of the creased vellum in the Ellesmere Chaucer may find its solution.

the Pardoner, fol. 138r

The presence of eight flyleaves is unusual enough to call for some comment and is an additional but quite minor expression of the lavishness which characterizes every aspect of the Ellesmere Chaucer. The amount of vellum squandered on these flyleaves would be sufficient for thirty-two pages of text in a folio manuscript, a not inconsiderable matter because vellum was usually one of the most expensive items in the making of the average medieval manuscript. This would point to a "de luxe" edition, prepared for an occasion or a person of some importance, in which case cost would be of slight consideration. The eight leaves are fully ruled in the same manner as the main body of text. Since the first and last of these leaves were originally pasted against the oak boards of the binding as endpapers and so required no ruling, it appears that they may not have been expressly prepared for the purpose they later served. Although three texts were subsequently written on them—the De Vere poem, a table of contents to the *Canterbury Tales* which adds the titles such as "The Marchant / Of Ianuarie and May. The Nonnes Preest / Of Chaunteclere and Pertelote," and Chaucer's poem "Truth" without envoi—these were all added at a substantially later date, and their inclusion here could not have been anticipated by the person responsible for adding the ruled blank leaves when the volume was originally bound. The puzzle is aggravated by the absence of any creases such as appear throughout the rest of the manuscript. The vellum itself is quite similar to the main body of text but appears to be very slightly heavier.

The manuscript is written in an English vernacular bookhand [anglicana formata], typical of the period and of this kind of literary text, and suggestive of the type used by Caxton for his printing of the *Canterbury Tales*, ca. 1478, as well as for other early English books. The scribe was a skilled writer but had a pronounced tendency, when he interrupted his copying at intervals to sharpen his quill pen or stir up his bottle of ink, or to call it the end of a satisfactory day's work, then to resume his task with a rather abrupt change in the size of the letters, the shade of the ink, or the bite of the pen nib. His identity is unknown, a customary misfortune experienced by students of medieval manuscripts; but it has been thought that he also wrote the text of another *Canterbury Tales*, the Hengwrt manuscript. The latter is also an excellent text, less subject to errors than the Ellesmere Chaucer, but less well organized as a complete and consecutive series of tales with proper connecting links between them. The Hengwrt manuscript, moreover, omits the Canon Yeoman's Prologue and Tale completely.

BIBLIOGRAPHICAL NOTE

by Joseph A. Dane and Seth Lerer

ERBERT C. SCHULZ worked at the Huntington Library for more than forty years and was curator of manuscripts from 1940 until his retirement in 1971. He was in a unique position to study the Ellesmere manuscript and we have reprinted his 1966 description above with only minor changes; these involve one or two omissions (noted by ellipses) and the addition of a few notes by M. B. Parkes made in Schulz's own typescript now in the Huntington archives (these are bracketed). We have taken the liberty of rewriting his concluding "Bibliographical Note" here.

The most important work on the Ellesmere manuscript during Schulz's tenure was the description of the manuscript made by John M. Manly and Edith Rickert for their 1940 *The Text of the "Canterbury Tales,"* a work Schulz several times refers to as "definitive." The Manly-Rickert edition dominated discussion of the *Canterbury Tales* text and its manuscripts through the 1940s and 1950s. Schulz's own three-page description of the manuscript history—one of the clearest narratives of that complex history available—seems to take entire phrases from this work. Nonetheless, Manly and Rickert explicitly thank Schulz for his "untiring aid", and it is quite likely that their influential description of the Ellesmere manuscript was in large part a product of discussions with Schulz himself. Schulz in 1966 is borrowing from the Manly-Rickert edition language that had been his own in 1940.

CHAUCER PORTRAIT, WOODCUT BY W. H. HOOPER (1872)

One major concern in Schulz's pamphlet and in his "Bibliographical Note" was the history of past reproductions of the
images from the manuscript. The first of these was the engraved
reproduction of Chaucer's equestrian portrait in Todd's 1810
Illustration of the Lives and Writings of Gower and Chaucer. There
followed the color woodcut reproductions by Hooper for the
Chaucer Society (1872), woodcut images often reprinted. In
1911, the Egerton family arranged to have the entire manuscript
reproduced in facsimile by the University Press of Manchester.
The 1911 facsimile itself is excellent by standards of the day, but
the colors are by modern standards flat and almost cartoonish.
Early reviewers noted also that the pages had been photographed
with multiple plates, and the relation of Pilgrim portraits to text
occasionally altered. Our own optical collations show that the
distortion is even more extensive, involving not only the relation
of portraits and colored borders to text, but also the relation
between portions of text on the same page. Furthermore, in all

CHAUCER PORTRAIT, FROM 1911 FACSIMILE

but the initial pages (which do not contain any text or illumination), the background has been reproduced as a featureless brown;
the marginal pricking marks, used to block out lines of text, are
gone, as are all indications of texture. The appearance is quite different from the three-dimensional surface characteristic of the
pages of manuscripts and early printed books in general and the
white pages of the Ellesmere manuscript in particular.

These touched-up facsimile images were then the source for
numerous reproductions of the images until mid-century (for
example, those by Piper in 1924). The Huntington archives contain an amusing exchange between Roger S. Loomis and Henry E.
Huntington from 1918. Loomis, who would become one of the
foremost American medievalists, writes for permission to photo-
graph some of the images from Huntington's newly acquired
manuscript and receives a curt reply from "HEH" dated 19 January
1918: "Dear Sir: In answer to your letter of the 21st, I would say
that in time the whole of the Bridgewater Chaucer will be repro-

duced for use by the public." By Huntington standards, 1965 was apparently not "in time"; Loomis, now near death, was still waiting, and reproduced from the 1911 facsimile the images for his *Mirror of Chaucer's World*.

In the 1970s, numerous facsimile projects for medieval manuscripts were underway, one by Pilgrim Books of Oklahoma—a project that produced a number of black-and-white facsimiles of key Chaucer manuscripts. These include a modest one-volume facsimile of the Hengwrt manuscript and a lavish black-and-white facsimile of Cambridge University MS.Gg.4.27, the first attempt at a complete works of Chaucer. The Cambridge manuscript contains several color portraits of the Canterbury Pilgrims, all reproduced in color in the facsimile. As the Huntington prepared to produce its own color facsimile of the Ellesmere manuscript, Ralph Hanna III published in 1989 an interesting "facsimile of a facsimile"—a black-and-white photographic reproduction, not of the Ellesmere manuscript itself, but of the 1911 facsimile. His introduction offered a sustained discussion of the practical and theoretical problems associated with such facsimile production.

As known to Schulz, the Ellesmere manuscript was bound in a full green morocco binding by Riviere & Son. This binding had been erroneously dated as early nineteenth century by Manly and Rickert. In 1966 Schulz noted that the name "Riviere & Son" was not used before 1880 and that the binding must be later than that date. It remained for both Ralph Hanna and Consuelo Dutschke to draw the logical conclusion that the binding should be dated 1911; the occasion for this binding was obviously the 1911 facsimile project itself—a project that had involved disbinding the manuscript into loose sheets prior to photographing them.

The color facsimile of the Ellesmere manuscript published jointly by the Huntington Library and Yushodo Co. Ltd. of Japan in 1995 is the most important event in the modern history of the manuscript. A volume of essays edited by Martin Stevens and

Daniel Woodward was published in 1995 to accompany this color facsimile. Some additional notes of ownership, unknown to Schulz, had been coaxed out of the pages with ultraviolet light by Ian Doyle, and the history of provenance further clarified by Hanna and A. S. G. Edwards in their study of the poem on the flyleaf in a special issue of *Huntington Library Quarterly* (1996).

The Huntington project involved disbinding the manuscript again and provided an opportunity for detailed study that had never been available for Schulz. The process was meticulously described and a detailed record of traces of earlier binding prepared by Anthony G. Cains, whose report appears in summary in the Stevens and Woodward volume and in full in the special issue of *Huntington Library Quarterly* noted above. The color facsimile, one of the most elaborate and lavish ever produced of a medieval manuscript, was published in 1995; in 1997, this facsimile was made available in a monochromatic version, which in itself is of some interest. It has been produced with far less contrast than is usual with black-and-white facsimiles, and the result is that viewers can see details of texture in the vellum pages—features that are readily apparent in manuscripts but often lost in the high-contrast photography characteristic of many competing projects.

Since 1966 there have been several major editorial projects on the *Canterbury Tales*. For Schulz, the primary editorial project had been the 1940 edition by Manly and Rickert. The assumptions, methods, and even conclusions of Manly and Rickert had been hotly debated during the 1950s, and to Schulz, the edition seemed to favor two manuscripts: the Ellesmere and Hengwrt manuscripts. Among Schulz's contemporary Chaucerians, a consensus seemed to be forming that the Ellesmere manuscript had been overrated in editorial history and that the best text of Chaucer's *Canterbury Tales* was to be found in the more modest Hengwrt manuscript. Various recent editions reflect this view: the 1958 edition by E. T. Donaldson and the 1980 edition by N. F. Blake both favor the Hengwrt manuscript, as does the multivolume Variorum Chaucer edition from Oklahoma University Press begun in 1979. But many scholars are skeptical. Thus, the 1987 Riverside edition edited by Larry D. Benson, the major Chaucer edition used in American universities, follows an editorial history based on Ellesmere. The first serious attempt to review the manuscript data collected by Manly and Rickert is now underway in the *Canterbury Tales* project from Cambridge University Press. The goal is to present each separate tale or prologue on a single CD-ROM, and to present on that CD-ROM images and transcriptions of all manuscript versions. A number of those images are available on the project's Web site (www.cup. org/Chaucer/ctptop.html). Many scholars believe that while the Ellesmere text can no longer be claimed to be definitive, no substitute text or authority has replaced it.

Reproductions of Images Before 1966

Text After that of H. C. Schulz

Henry J. Todd, *Illustrations of the Lives and Writings of Gower and Chaucer* (London, 1810). The frontispiece is an engraving of the Chaucer equestrian portrait.

A Six-Text Print of Chaucer's Canterbury Tales in Parallel Columns, ed. F. J. Furnivall, Chaucer Society Publications, ser. 1, 15 (London, 1871) and 25 (1872). Woodcuts by W. H. Hooper of all the paintings in the Ellesmere manuscript, in color, are reproduced in these volumes. The same cuts, uncolored, are in *The Ellesmere Manuscript of Chaucer's "Canterbury Tales,"* ed. Furnivall, Chaucer Society Publications ser., 1, 16 (1871), and 26 (1872).

The Ellesmere Chaucer Reproduced in Facsimile, 2 vols. (Manchester, 1911). The pages with borders are reproduced in color other pages in black-and-white. The paintings that are smudged in the manuscript (the Miller, the Man of Law, the Monk, and the Nun's Priest) have been retouched.

E. E. Piper, "The Miniatures of the Ellesmere Chaucer," *Philological Quarterly*, 3 (1924): 241–56. The illustrations are reproduced from the 1911 facsimile edition.

Roger S. Loomis, *A Mirror of Chaucer's World* (Princeton, 1965). The illustration of Chaucer is from the manuscript, the remaining figures from the facsimile edition.

OTHER MANUSCRIPT ILLUSTRATIONS

Guthrie Vine, "The Miller's Tale," *John Rylands Library Bulletin*, 27 (1933): 333–47. Reproduces the figure of the Miller from the "Oxford" manuscript, two leaves of which are in the Rylands Library (Rylands English MS 63).

The Rosenbach Company, *An Exhibition of Fifteenth Century Manuscripts and Books in Honour of the Six Hundredth Anniversary of the Birth of Geoffrey Chaucer* (New York, 1940). Reproduces the figure of the Cook from the "Oxford" manuscript, eleven leaves of which are owned by the Rosenbach Foundation, Philadelphia (Rosenbach, 1084.2). The other figure, the Manciple, is not reproduced.

ADDITIONAL REFERENCES
(text by the editors):

Theo Stemmler, ed., *The Ellesmere Miniatures of the Canterbury Pilgrims* (Mannheim, 1976). Pilgrim portraits are reproduced as photographs, rather than prints; sizes are "equalized."

Paul G. Ruggiers, ed., The Canterbury Tales: *A Facsimile and Transcription of the Hengwrt Manuscript* (Norman, Okla., 1979). Black-and-white facsimile; Ellesmere variants included in the transcription.

M. B. Parkes and Richard Beadle, eds., *Geoffrey Chaucer: Poetical Works, a Facsimile of Cambridge University Library MS. Gg. 4.27* (Norman, Okla., 1980). Black-and-white facsimile; portraits reproduced in color.

Ralph Hanna III, *The Ellesmere Manuscript of Chaucer's* Canterbury Tales: *A Working Facsimile* (Cambridge, 1989).

C. W. Dutschke, *Guide to Medieval and Renaissance Manuscripts in the Huntington Library*, 2 vols. (San Marino, Calif., 1989).

Daniel Woodward and Martin Stevens, eds., The Canterbury Tales *(ca. 1410): The New Ellesmere Chaucer Facsimile* (Tokyo and San Marino, Calif., 1995); *The New Ellesmere Chaucer Monochromatic Facsimile* (San Marino, Calif., 1997).

Martin Stevens and Daniel Woodward, eds., *The Ellesmere Chaucer: Essays in Interpretation* (San Marino, Calif., 1995).

Seth Lerer, ed., *Reading from the Margins: Textual Studies, Chaucer, and Medieval Literature* (special issue of *Huntington Library Quarterly*, 58, no. 1 (1996) (San Marino, Calif., 1996).

Fle fro the prees and dwell with soothfastnesse
Suffise vn to thi good though it be smal
For hord hath hate and clymbynge tikelnesse
Prees hath envye and wele blyndeth ouer al
Sauo no more than the by houe shal
Werke wel thi selfe that other folke canst rede
And trouthe shal delyue it is no drede

Tempest the noght al croked to redresse
In trust of hir that turneth as a balle
For gret reste stant in litel bisinesse
And ek be war to sporne agayn an al
Stryue noght as doth the crokke with the wal
Daunt thi self that dauntest otheres dede
And trouthe shal delyue it is no drede

That the is sent receyue in boxomnesse
The wrastlynge for this worlde axeth a fal
Her nis non hom her nis but wildernesse
Forth pilgrym forth forth beste out of thi stal
Knowe thi contree lok vp thank god of al
Holde the hie wey and lat thi gost the lede
And trouthe shal delyue it is no drede

Man be ware and bel auysid · sey noo thyng but zefen and sey!
To speke of thyng that ben dissprysid · I holde yt foly euy sey!
They was a noyne that mon del knede

for thine horne

Quid sis quid fuis quid eris semp memor eris

agayn be ware the way ys slider thy soule shall to thow wate

Quisquis amas mundum tibi prospice quo sit eundum
hec ma qua vidis via pessima plenaq cladis

Holde euly sere yd hyraty

fortune that yatz yate and clymbyng tikelnes
prese hath envm and is el blynd the ou alt